D1487279

It's Your Health!

Smoking

JUDITH ANDERSON

A⁺
Smart Apple Media

First published in 2004 by Franklin Watts
96 Leonard Street, London EC2A 4XD

Franklin Watts Australia
45–51 Huntley Street, Alexandria NSW 2015

Series editor: Sarah Peutrill, Designed by: Pewter Design Associates, Series design: Peter Scoulding, Illustration: Mike Atkinson and Guy Smith, Mainline Design, Picture researcher: Diana Morris, Series consultant: Wendy Anthony, Health Education Unit, Education Service, Birmingham City Council

Picture credits: Jerry Arcieri/Corbis: 8c. Paul Baldesare/Photofusion. Posed by models: front cover. Baumgartner Olivia/Corbis Sygma: 41cr. Norm Betts/Rex Features: 33bl. Richard Bickel/Corbis: 8bl. Ed Bock/Corbis: 20b. BSIP, Alexandre/SPL: 23c. BSIP, Laurent/SPL: 21b. Alexander Caminada/Rex Features: 24c. Mark Clarke/SPL: 11tr. Stuart Clarke/Rex Features: 25b. Pablo Corral/Corbis: 30t. Deep Light/SPL:19t. Colin Edwards/Photofusion: 34t. Chris Fairclough: 4, 9, 14, 36, 41, 45. Owen Franken/Corbis: 16b. A. Glauberman/SPL:18c. Paul Hardy/Corbis: 17b. Hayley Madden/S.I.N./Corbis: 40c. Faye Norman/SPL: 22c. Claire Paxton & Jacqui Farrow/SPL: 26c. Mark Peterson/Corbis: 29b, 31b. Harvey Pincis/SPL: 12c. James Prince/SPL: 35c. Joel W. Rogers/Corbis: 28b. Saturn Stills/SPL: 37t. Chuck Savage/Corbis: 39c. Christopher Smith/Corbis: 23b. Roman Soumar/Corbis: 29t. Stapleton Collection, UK/Bridgeman Art Library: 10b. Tom Stewart/Corbis: 38c. James A. Sugar/Corbis: 21c. Swim Ink/Corbis: 11b. Charles Sykes/Rex Features: 32b. Tek Image/SPL: 13bl. Jonathan Torgovnik/Corbis: 27t. Nik Wheeler/Corbis: 31t. Richard Young/Rex Features: 15c.

Published in the United States by Smart Apple Media
2140 Howard Drive West, North Mankato, Minnesota 56003

U.S. publication copyright © 2006 Smart Apple Media

Printed in the United States of America

Library of Congress Cataloging-in-Publication Data

Anderson, Judith.
Smoking / by Judith Anderson.
p. cm. — (It's your health)
Includes index.
ISBN 1-58340-587-9
1. Smoking—Juvenile literature. I. Title. II. Series.

QP801.T57A535 2005
613.85—dc22   2004056457

9 8 7 6 5 4 3 2 1

Contents

What is tobacco?

Tobacco is made from the dried leaves of the tobacco plant. The tobacco plant is a member of the same botanical family as potatoes and tomatoes. It is grown in more than 100 countries around the world and processed into a variety of products, including cigarettes, cigars, pipe tobacco, "chew" tobacco, and snuff. Of these, cigarettes are by far the most popular.

The world's 1.2 billion smokers smoke about 20 billion cigarettes every day.

Cigarettes

Cigarettes are made from dried tobacco, paper, a variety of additives, and, in most cases, a filter. Hand-rolled cigarettes may not have a filter. When a cigarette is lit, the tobacco breaks down into ash and smoke. The smoker inhales the smoke through the filter into the throat and lungs.

According to the tobacco industry, tobacco creates more employment per acre of cultivated land than any other crop in the world.

It's your experience

"I don't see what all the fuss is about. My parents and my brother smoke, but I don't mind. Everyone does it. I think there are far more important problems in the world."

Sam, age 12

Nicotine

Tobacco contains nicotine. Nicotine is a type of drug known as a "stimulant" because it stimulates the central nervous system, increasing the heart rate and raising blood pressure.

Nicotine is an addictive drug, which means that smokers may suffer withdrawal symptoms when they don't have it. It is also poisonous if taken in large amounts. Nevertheless, nicotine is a legal drug in every country in the world.

Additives

The tobacco in cigarettes contains a wide range of additives such as preservatives and flavorings. These additives are not listed as ingredients on cigarette packs but are generally designed to keep the tobacco fresh, to mask any unpleasant taste or smell, and to increase the appeal to smokers.

In some countries, more than 600 additives are allowed to be added to cigarettes. Some people think that not enough is known about the health effects of these additives.

Oral tobacco

Not all tobacco users smoke cigarettes. In India and parts of Africa and Southeast Asia, people chew dried tobacco leaves (*areca*) or a mixture of tobacco, leaves, and spices (*betel quids*). The leaves are chewed to release the juices, and the rest is spit out.

Oral tobacco avoids health problems associated with smoke, but users cannot avoid the dangers of nicotine addiction and the powerful cancer-causing compounds known as nitrosamines that are present in all tobacco. Research indicates that oral tobacco users are 50 times more likely to develop oral, cancer. Despite this fact, the use of oral or, "spit," tobacco is on the increase among young males in the United States.

It's your decision

Are you concerned about the environment? Some antismoking campaigners think that people who decide to smoke should be more aware of the environmental consequences. They say that the production of tobacco involves the intensive use of pesticides and pollution from toxic chemical waste. Tobacco production is also responsible for approximately one-eighth of the world's deforestation, since trees are cut down to provide fuel for the drying process.

▼ Do we know exactly what we are smoking?

The history of smoking

Historians believe that Native Americans began using tobacco for medicinal and ceremonial purposes more than 2,000 years ago. However, tobacco was not introduced into Europe until Spanish and Portuguese explorers brought it back from the Americas at the end of the 15th century.

Snuff, cigars, and cigarettes

At first, tobacco was smoked in pipes, but by the end of the 17th century, the sniffing of powdered tobacco, called "snuff," was becoming increasingly widespread. Cigars became fashionable among the wealthy in the 19th century, and poor people soon learned to save the tobacco from discarded stubs in order to re-roll it between strips of paper. This became the cigarette.

The 20th century

Cigarettes became increasingly popular as industrial production methods and more efficient means of distribution made them cheaper and easier to buy. By the outbreak of World War I in 1914, smoking had become a mass habit. Tobacco companies such as Philip Morris in the U.S. and British American Tobacco in Britain expanded rapidly and began to sell their products in new markets overseas.

Snuff use was a social habit enjoyed by the wealthy in the 18th century.

During World War II (1939–45), U.S. soldiers were issued cigarettes as part of their rations. In the 1940s, about 65 percent of men and 41 percent of women in Britain were smokers.

Since the 1960s, smoking rates among adults in developed countries have generally declined. However, in many developing countries in the Far East and Africa, smoking is on the increase.

It's your experience

> "When I was a girl, my brother told me that smoking helped to keep colds away. We all smoked back then. I know it is bad for me, but I've lasted this long, and I am not going to quit now."
>
> Margaret, age 94

"FIFTY-FIFTY ON MY LAST SMOKE, BILL!"

Mail Your Contributions to

"OUR BOYS IN FRANCE TOBACCO FUND"

West 44th Street   Endorsed by War Department   New York City

A poster from 1918 asks Americans to support the war effort by sending cigarettes to the troops in World War I.

Research into smoking

The ill-effects of smoking on the throat and lungs were noted as early as the 17th century. However, many people insisted on the medicinal qualities of tobacco, and smoking was not publicly linked to cancer until 1951.

Researchers began to investigate the chemical content of cigarette smoke, but the tobacco industry disputed their findings and refused to accept that nicotine was addictive. Nevertheless, some governments began to listen to the advice of antismoking campaigners. The first health warning appeared on cigarette packages in the U.S. in 1965, in Britain in 1971, and in Australia in 1972.

It's your opinion

◆ Why do you think tobacco companies were reluctant to accept that nicotine is addictive?
◆ Why might smoking be on the rise in developing countries?

What happens when we smoke?

When we inhale, or breathe in, a lighted cigarette, the burning tobacco reaches temperatures of up to 1290 °F (700 °C) at the tip. This causes a number of chemical reactions to take place, including the formation of gases such as carbon monoxide and of tiny droplets of sticky solids, known as tar.

Tobacco smoke contains about 4,000 chemical compounds. Many are present in tiny, insignificant amounts, but some are more toxic and are known to cause cancer.

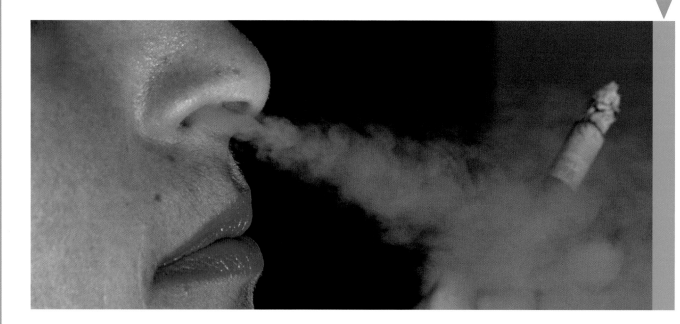

In the lungs

When we draw tobacco smoke into our lungs, it irritates the delicate lining of the air passages, which may make us cough or experience a burning sensation. The brown, syrupy tar condenses and sticks to the walls of our bronchioles and alveoli. This interferes with the lungs' ability to fight infection and makes us more vulnerable to colds, flu, bronchitis, and pneumonia. It also makes it more difficult for oxygen to pass from the lungs into the bloodstream. Some of the tar remains in our lungs, but the rest is gradually absorbed through the lung walls.

It's your experience

"The first time I smoked was awful. I thought my throat was burning, and I felt really sick. I got used to it pretty quickly, though. And I liked the buzz it gave me. But now when I light up, I don't feel anything at all."

Jack, age 18

In the bloodstream

Once the chemicals from tobacco smoke get into our bloodstream, they are transported rapidly through the body. Carbon monoxide reduces the amount of oxygen in the blood because it binds with hemoglobin in red blood cells more easily than oxygen does. This makes our heart and lungs work harder. It can also reduce our ability to think quickly.

In the brain

It takes between 8 and 15 seconds for nicotine to travel from our lungs to the brain. Nicotine stimulates the receptors in the brain, which increases our heart rate and blood pressure and generates feelings of pleasure. This is the dizzy sensation, or smoking "high," that new smokers experience.

Smoke enters the airway through the nose and mouth

The brain receives a "high"

Tar is deposited in the lungs

Nicotine and carbon monoxide pass through the lung walls and into the bloodstream

▲ Smoking affects your lungs, blood, and brain.

▼ Special machines "smoke" cigarettes to test their chemical content.

It's your decision

▶ High tar, low tar, or no tar?
Some of us choose to buy cigarettes labeled "low in tar." This usually means that they have a perforated filter that allows air to mix with cigarette smoke. However, antismoking campaigners argue that addicted smokers compensate for lower levels of nicotine by smoking more cigarettes or inhaling more deeply.

13

Why do people start smoking?

Most people start smoking between the ages of 11 and 15. In the U.S. and Britain, more than 80 percent of adult smokers began smoking in their teens.

Why so young?

There are many reasons why young people start smoking, ranging from curiosity, the influence of other smokers in the family, rebellion, or pressure from friends to the belief that smoking is cool or exciting. For some of us, it is the desire to be part of a group, while for others, it is about breaking away from the safety of childhood.

There is also growing evidence to suggest that advertising projects an image of smoking that is particularly attractive to young people (see pages 28–29).

Family and friends

We are all influenced by what other people think and do. There is nothing wrong with this, but it can become a problem if we are under too much pressure to behave in a certain way. The tobacco industry argues that smoking among young people is a societal problem. It insists that most smokers take up the habit as a result of family or peer pressure.

Certainly, children are more likely to smoke if both of their parents smoke, and numerous studies have shown that most young smokers are influenced by their friends' and older siblings' smoking habits.

Older friends and siblings can influence smoking habits. ▼

It's your experience

▶ "I go into town every Saturday with a group of friends from school. They all smoke, but at first I didn't want to. Then my friends started talking about going without me, so I started smoking, too. I know it's not good for me but I don't want to be left out."

Emma, age 14

It's your decision

▶ Are you adventurous?
The tobacco company Philip Morris has suggested that the decision to start smoking is a symbolic act. "I am no longer my mother's child, I'm tough, I am an adventurer, I'm not square. . . . As the force from the psychological symbolism subsides, the pharmacological [drug] effect takes over to sustain the habit."

 Images like this suggest that smoking is glamorous and fun.

Influence of the media

Films, television, music, and magazines are good at creating the image of a lifestyle we would like to have. When a film star or a famous model lights a cigarette, it looks glamorous. A recent World Health Organization survey has examined the Indian film industry and found that young people who watch their favorite actors smoke are three times more likely to do so themselves. The survey also found that these same young people are 16 times more likely to think positively about smoking.

Addiction

People start smoking for many different reasons, but most continue to smoke for one reason only—they are addicted to nicotine. Addiction occurs when we take a drug that changes the way we feel and on which we become increasingly dependent, both in order to continue to experience its effects and to avoid the discomfort of its absence.

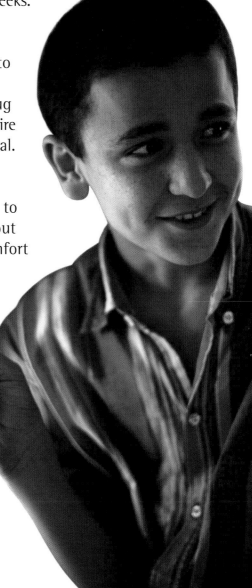

In many developing countries, young people have little access to information about addiction.

Rapid addiction

It is not only long-term smokers who are addicted to nicotine. Children who smoke as little as one cigarette a day can show signs of physical dependence after just four weeks.

The nicotine effect

The addictive effect of nicotine is linked to its capacity to trigger the release of dopamine—a chemical in the brain that is associated with feelings of pleasure. Once the drug wears off, we want another cigarette. For many, this desire comes from an addiction that is both mental and physical.

Physical addiction

Physical addiction occurs when our bodies become used to having a certain amount of nicotine in the blood. Without further doses of nicotine, we begin to experience discomfort in the form of withdrawal symptoms such as irritability, restlessness, anxiety, and even depression.

It's your decision

Will cigarettes help you concentrate? Many smokers believe that cigarettes help them concentrate, but research suggests that the only thing cigarettes do is temporarily suppress the withdrawal symptoms caused by not smoking.

Mental addiction

Mental addiction occurs because nicotine is both stimulating and relaxing. Over time, we learn to use these effects to cope with negative feelings and emotions such as boredom or stress. We develop a psychological dependence.

Habit-forming

Smoking is often referred to as a "habit," and this, too, is a form of mental addiction, as our brains learn to associate smoking with specific activities, such as having a drink or watching TV. These habits can be very hard to break.

It's your experience

"I've been smoking since I was 15. My urge to smoke is triggered by all sorts of things like stress and tiredness or eating or relaxing. Watching someone else light up makes me want a cigarette. Even talking about smoking creates a craving."

Paul, age 43

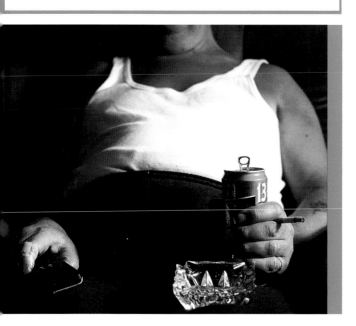

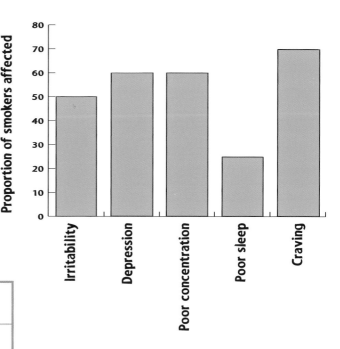

Symptoms of addiction to nicotine: proportion of smokers affected

Proportion of smokers affected

80 70 60 50 40 30 20 10 0

Irritability — Depression — Poor concentration — Poor sleep — Craving

Symptom of addiction to nicotine

Difficulty quitting

Nicotine is a powerfully addictive drug. Surveys show that at least 70 percent of smokers want to stop smoking. Yet, only about three percent are able to quit by using willpower alone, and few smokers believe that they could go an entire day without a cigarette. Some scientists argue that nicotine is as addictive as illegal drugs such as heroin and cocaine.

Some people, particularly young women, don't want to quit because they believe that smoking helps suppress their appetite.

◀ Drinking alcohol and watching TV trigger the urge to smoke in many people.

Smoking and disease

We all have been told that smoking is bad for us. Nevertheless, most of us prefer to think that we can stop smoking before disease takes hold. According to statistics, this is a mistaken belief. About half of all regular smokers will eventually be killed by the habit.

Nonfatal diseases

Even if smoking does not prove fatal, smokers are more likely to suffer from an impaired immune system and a wide range of nonfatal illnesses such as impotence, psoriasis, hearing problems, cough, chest pain, and gum disease. They may also have bad breath, stained fingers, and yellow teeth.

Cancer

Cigarette smoke contains at least 60 carcinogens, or cancer-causing compounds. Carcinogens are absorbed through the mouth, throat, and lungs, which is why cancers in these parts of the body are most commonly found in smokers. It is estimated that more than 80 percent of all deaths from lung cancer are due to smoking. However, the carcinogens also leak into our bloodstream and cause cancers in other organs, including the bladder, kidneys, stomach, and pancreas.

The lung specimen on the right is from a smoker, while the one on the left is from a nonsmoker. The smoker's lung is darker, rougher, and misshapen.

Heart disease and stroke

A smoker is two to three times more likely to have a heart attack than a nonsmoker is. This is because smoking affects the steady supply of blood to the heart.

Nicotine raises blood pressure by causing blood vessels to contract, forcing the heart to work harder, while carbon monoxide reduces the heart's effectiveness by lowering the amount of oxygen in the blood. Smoking also thickens the walls of arteries and makes blood clot, which may lead to a sudden blockage, resulting in a heart attack or stroke.

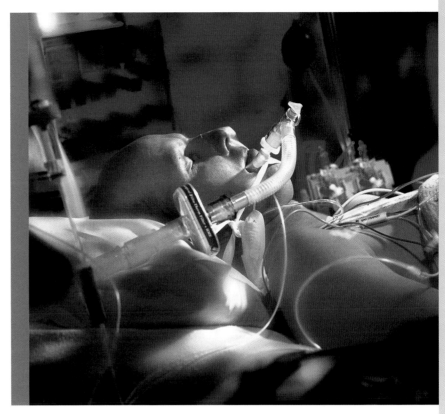

This man is breathing with the aid of a respirator after heart surgery. Smoking causes 25 percent of deaths from heart disease.

Divided opinion

Over the last decade, growing numbers of smokers who have contracted lung disease have tried to sue tobacco companies. The tobacco industry has argued that the impact of smoking on the health of a specific individual is too difficult to assess and that health warnings have been printed on cigarette packs for more than 40 years.

It's your opinion

Do you think smokers are justified in seeking compensation from tobacco companies?

It's your decision

Do you want to start smoking now? The younger we are when we decide to smoke, the more dangerous it is. Someone who starts smoking at the age of 15 is 3 times more likely to die of cancer due to smoking than someone who starts in his or her mid-20s. This is partly because a younger person is likely to smoke for a greater number of years, but recent studies have also indicated that smoking in our teens can cause permanent genetic changes in the lungs that increase the risk of lung cancer.

Smoking and sports

Smoking affects our physical performance. All major sporting organizations advise people who participate in sports not to smoke. In the long term, continued smoking damages our lungs and puts a strain on our hearts, making exercise difficult.

Can a smoker reach the peak of physical fitness?

Less energy

When we exercise, our muscles require more oxygen. Our lungs and heart need to work efficiently in order to supply this oxygen and to remove carbon dioxide from the body.

Yet, when we smoke, the nicotine makes our arteries contract, while the carbon monoxide we inhale reduces the amount of oxygen our blood can absorb. Our muscles have less energy. We tire more quickly and become more breathless than we would if we had not had a cigarette. Nevertheless, a smoker who exercises regularly is likely to be in better health than a smoker who never exercises at all.

Secret smokers

Very few athletes who are competing at the top level admit to smoking. Most do not smoke, but for some, the addictive power of nicotine is so great that they continue to smoke, despite the risk to their physical performance and their mental concentration. The pressure on them as role models means that they are too afraid of disappointing fans and attracting criticism to admit to their addiction.

Sponsorship

Most sporting events are funded by sponsors that promote their products and services at the event. Tobacco companies like to sponsor sports because they are watched by millions of people on TV and because sports have an image of adventure and success that corresponds with the image of many cigarette brands.

The European Union is banning all tobacco-related sponsorship of sports in its member countries because it believes that such sponsorship encourages young people to take up the habit. However, some people argue that as a result, events such as Formula 1 racing will relocate to countries such as China where there are fewer restrictions and greater numbers of potential smokers.

It's your experience

"I have never had a problem with our young players smoking. They are all aware of the health risks, and none of them want to jeopardize their place on the team."

Head coach of the academy at Manchester United Football Club

A sports fan celebrates with a cigar. In some countries, tobacco is given away free at sports events.

It's your opinion

Sponsorship deals mean more money for sports. Do you think tobacco companies should be allowed to sponsor events such as Formula 1 racing?

This girl is breathing into a machine called a spirometer to measure her lung capacity.

Secondhand smoke

When a cigarette is lit, smoke from the burning tip combines with the smoker's exhaled smoke to form what is known as secondhand smoke. Antismoking groups have been concerned about the effects of secondhand smoke for more than 30 years.

Is it harmful?

Many studies have been published to suggest that people exposed to secondhand smoke face some of the same risks faced by smokers, including lung cancer and heart disease. However, the evidence has been hotly disputed, and tobacco companies maintain that while passive smoking may be unpleasant, it has not been proved to damage people's health.

Many children are exposed to secondhand smoke in their homes. ▼

Secondhand smoke and children

According to the World Health Organization, almost half of the world's children are exposed to other people's tobacco smoke. For young children, this smoke is mainly from parents and other family members in the home. This raises serious health issues because many studies have found a link between secondhand smoke and asthma, bronchitis, pneumonia, and middle-ear infections in children.

Pregnancy

Unborn children are also affected by secondhand smoke. When a pregnant woman smokes, the chemicals in her blood pass into the bloodstream of the fetus. This is believed to contribute to low birth weight and Sudden Infant Death Syndrome (SIDS) in young babies.

▼ Smoking while pregnant can cause the baby to be smaller than average and can reduce its chances of survival.

Public places

Bans on smoking in public places are becoming increasingly common, particularly in developed countries. In New York, smoking is now banned in all restaurants with more than 35 seats and in almost all buildings used by the public. In Britain, there are now nonsmoking areas on some beaches.

However, it is difficult to measure the health benefits of such bans. They are popular with nonsmokers, but the owners of restaurants and bars often worry that a smoking ban may lead to a decrease in the number of customers. Even some nonsmokers say that people should be allowed to smoke in bars.

It's your decision

Pro-smoking campaigners argue that to ban smoking in public places is to deny smokers their right to personal freedom. Antismoking campaigners argue that smoking in public places denies nonsmokers their right to a healthy environment. Whose rights matter more?

▲ Patrons of a New York bar have to smoke outside.

The law

Many countries have laws to protect children from the dangers of smoking. Some countries have also taken steps to increase public awareness about tobacco and its effects. The U.S. and the European Union have passed laws requiring clearer labeling of the nicotine and tar content of cigarettes, more explicit health warnings, and less advertising. However, in some parts of the world, cigarettes are not so heavily regulated.

This clerk refuses to sell a child cigarettes, but some retailers ignore the law.

The law and young people

Many laws about smoking are intended to prevent young people from taking up the habit. In Britain, it is illegal for anyone to sell cigarettes to a person who appears to be younger than 16. A retailer can be fined up to $1,800 if caught. In Australia, the legal age for smoking is 18, and fines for retailers can be much higher. In many states in the U.S., it is illegal for people younger than 18 to possess or use tobacco, and young people are fined if they are caught with it.

Taxes

Most countries tax the sale of tobacco, which means that an additional charge must be included in the price of every pack of cigarettes. In some countries, this tax amounts to as much as 80 percent of the total cost of a pack of cigarettes.

Taxing tobacco sales has two purposes: to raise revenue for the government and to reduce smoking. The World Bank concludes that when the price of cigarettes increases, consumption falls.

Smuggling

Some people try to avoid paying these higher taxes. Smugglers illegally import cigarettes on which they have paid no tax and sell them at hugely discounted prices.

Smuggled cigarettes are a problem for the police and customs agencies. And the fact that they are much cheaper means that more young people will buy them.

It's your opinion

In New York in 2002, a judge ordered a woman not to smoke in her home or in her car because of the potential harm to her healthy son, who objected to tobacco smoke. Do you think this kind of legal intervention is acceptable?

It's your decision

The British government says, "We are not going to ban smoking. We accept that smokers have a right to choose to smoke, but we also have a responsibility to reduce smoking and save lives." The government tries to curb smoking by making it more and more expensive. Yet many people continue to smoke despite the cost.

This problem is made worse by the Internet. Cigarettes on which no tax has been paid can be bought online by young people who do not have to prove that they are old enough to smoke. Legislation in some countries is attempting to deal with this issue, but smuggling and tax evasion are likely to continue.

◁ Customs officials seize smuggled cigarettes and alcohol.

The costs of smoking

In addition to being expensive for individuals, smoking costs society as a whole, mainly through medical costs for smoking-related illnesses, the costs of house and forest fires, and business costs for time off of work. The actual cost is difficult to assess, however, because it must be balanced by income from taxation, donations by tobacco companies, and jobs and wealth created by the tobacco industry.

A doctor shows a young woman a brochure on quitting smoking. Society pays for both the prevention and treatment of smoking-related diseases.

It's your experience

"I don't know how much money I've spent on cigarettes over the last three years. I don't think I want to know."

Megan, age 17

Health costs and taxes

In the U.S., it has been estimated that each pack of cigarettes has a social cost of $3.45 because of the cost of treating smoking-related diseases. In Britain, the National Health Service spends $3 billion each year to treat the effects of smoking. These costs are often compared with the amount of tax raised by the government from the sale of cigarettes, which in Britain amounts to more than $16 billion.

Antismoking campaigners point out that taxes must be raised from somewhere, and research shows that raising the cost of cigarettes encourages smokers to quit. However, more nonsmokers means less tax for the government, and pro-smoking organizations argue that because smokers die younger than others, they actually cost the state less in medical expenses and social security payments.

Division of money spent on drug-related health problems in Australia, 2003

22% alcohol

61% smoking

17% illegal drugs

A young homeless boy smoking in India.

Industry and employment

Smoking is expensive for employers. Smoking-related illnesses result in time off of work, and smokers and their employers pay higher insurance costs. A Canadian study found that cigarette breaks cost employers more than $2,000 per smoker per year.

The tobacco industry counters that it employs more than 100 million people worldwide, but the World Bank states that with a global fall in tobacco consumption "more jobs are likely to be created than lost." The leisure and tourism industries in particular would benefit from more healthy, wealthy nonsmokers.

Smoking and poverty

Higher taxes on cigarettes may deter some of us from smoking, but the nature of addiction means that many people will continue to smoke. In developing countries, the cost of smoking can have a direct impact on malnutrition. A study in Bangladesh has shown that poorer people who smoke spend less on their family's food in order to pay for their habit.

It's your decision

Will smoking affect your job prospects?
If a nonsmoker and a smoker both apply for the same job, and the employer is aware that smokers generally take more time off of work, he or she is more likely to choose the nonsmoker.

Advertising

Tobacco companies advertise their products in many different ways. When permitted, they place advertisements in magazines, on television, on billboards, and in store windows. They may sponsor events, offer free gifts, and even pay to have their products smoked by celebrities. Many companies also place brand "reminders," such as stickers, at the point of sale in convenience stores and supermarkets.

The power of advertising

Tobacco companies have entered into agreements that regulate their advertising. Nevertheless, most of us are exposed to some form of tobacco advertising on a regular basis. The Campaign for Tobacco-Free Kids says that young people are three times more sensitive to tobacco advertisements than adults and that one-third of underage experimentation with smoking is due to tobacco ads.

Brand selling

The tobacco industry argues that peer pressure remains the biggest influence on first-time smokers and that advertising affects only the brand they choose.

In the U.S., more than 80 percent of young smokers prefer the three most heavily advertised brands, compared with less than half of adult smokers. This is because new young smokers are more influenced by image than by other factors such as price or taste.

Antismoking campaigners believe that "Joe Camel" encouraged underage smoking.

It's your opinion

Think about some of the tobacco advertisements you have come across recently. What do you remember about them? What message were they trying to get across? Did they have an impact on you?

◀ Tobacco advertisement on a wall in India.

Changing times

Some forms of tobacco advertising, such as billboards and sponsorship deals, are being outlawed, and TV advertising is not allowed in many countries, yet the tobacco industry knows it has to attract new smokers if it is to survive. When billboard advertisements were banned in the U.S., tobacco promotions in convenience stores increased. In most countries, tobacco companies can still place their cigarettes in films and trade unrelated goods such as clothes under cigarette brand names in order to advertise their products.

New restrictions on tobacco advertising are being introduced all the time, but loopholes remain, and in many of the biggest markets in Southeast Asia and Africa, there are very few restrictions at all.

It's your decision

Does advertising persuade you? Tobacco companies say that they do not aim their advertising at young nonsmokers. Antismoking campaigners disagree. They say that sophisticated adult-targeted advertising makes cigarettes even more appealing to children.

▲ Tobacco ads on the door of a convenience store.

The power of tobacco companies

Cigarettes mean big business for the handful of companies that dominate the global tobacco market. Their profits are huge, and their business is multinational—brands such as Marlboro are marketed around the world.

In Argentina, this man's sunhat becomes a marketing tool.

Misuse of power?

In the past, the tobacco industry has been accused of exploiting poor farmers, unfairly influencing government decisions about smoking policy, and covering up research about the damaging effects of cigarettes. However, in the light of the overwhelming evidence about the dangers of smoking, tobacco companies are now redefining themselves as socially responsible employers, funding youth smoking prevention programs, and establishing voluntary codes of conduct. British American Tobacco says, "We believe in adding value to the communities in which we operate."

Nevertheless, antismoking campaigners insist that the industry continues to misuse its power. Many tobacco companies have now diversified into other products, including food production and finance. This means that many people are investing in tobacco companies without realizing it.

Threats to the industry

In high-income countries, smoking among adults is generally declining. This is mainly due to better information about health issues, new restrictions on advertising, and high taxation. Some tobacco companies are being required to pay huge sums in compensation to smokers.

Fighting back

However, the tobacco industry's arguments for freedom of speech continue to influence many international trade agreements, and big tobacco companies are expanding into new markets in lower-income countries with fewer restrictions and less health awareness.

New recruits

In the developing world, approximately 48 percent of men and 7 percent of women currently smoke. Given the huge populations of countries such as China and India, a small increase in smoking among women would greatly increase the size of the world tobacco market.

Big tobacco companies are already tapping into this potential by promoting brands such as Virginia Slims as modern, sophisticated, and "western." The result is a new demand, especially among women and young people. By the mid-2020s, it is predicted that about 85 percent of the world's smokers will live in developing countries, which are least able to fight an epidemic of addiction and disease.

The World Health Organization has estimated that the number of women who smoke will almost triple over the next generation to more than 500 million.

It's your opinion

The U.S. has a Cigarette Advertising and Promotion Code to regulate the activities of the tobacco industry. In order to avoid imposing American values on other societies, this code is not applied to the activities of American tobacco companies in other countries. Antismoking campaigners think this is hypocritical. What do you think?

In 2000, Nottingham University received $6.8 million from British American Tobacco to fund an International Center for Corporate Social Responsibility. Some teachers and professors decided to resign in protest. Do you think they had a point?

Cigarette production at the R.J. Reynolds plant in North Carolina.

Antismoking campaigns

Antismoking campaigns are usually initiated by health workers, government policymakers, or pressure groups such as Action on Smoking and Health (ASH). Generally, they have one or more of three goals: to prevent young people from smoking, to persuade existing smokers to quit, and to protect people from the dangers of secondhand smoke.

Which ones work?

Different campaigns work better for different groups of people. Information "shocks," or widely publicized official reports on the dangers of smoking, tend to have the greatest impact where general awareness of the health risks is low. As knowledge increases, new information shocks become less effective, although they do continue to contribute to a general drop in smoking.

School programs

School antismoking programs are widespread, but while many young people who smoke remember health education lessons, they choose to ignore them. Researchers say this is because young people tend to be less influenced by information about the long-term effects of smoking and more concerned with rebellion against adult advice.

Some recent campaigns have focused on less life-threatening problems, such as yellow teeth, bad breath, and bad skin, in order to get their message across. The Australian government has sponsored a Smoke Free Fashion initiative to challenge the idea that smoking is fashionable and to avoid images that might encourage young people to smoke.

Film star Jackie Chan supports an antismoking rally in the U.S.

Graphic health warnings

Since the 1960s, a growing number of governments have required cigarette manufacturers to print health warnings on their products. These warnings vary from small printed messages to graphic color pictures of lung tumors, diseased hearts, and rotting teeth. In Canada, such images have covered the top half of both sides of cigarette packages since 2001, and 44 percent of smokers say this has increased their motivation to quit.

Such campaigns are likely to be less effective in poorer countries where cigarettes are often sold singly, instead of in packs.

It's your experience

▶ "I know that millions of people die every year from smoking, but I've never paid much attention to the statistics. I stopped when my boyfriend said my breath smelled bad."

Janine, age 16

Smoking kills

Smoking harms your baby

Smoking is highly addictive, don't start

Smoking seriously harms you and others around you

Smokers die younger

▲ Health warnings on cigarette packages are becoming harder to ignore.

It's your opinion

▶ What type of antismoking campaign is likely to influence you most, and why?

California: a case study

In 1988, California significantly raised tobacco taxes and spent 20 percent of the revenue on an aggressive public education campaign. Over the next decade, it banned smoking in public places such as offices and restaurants. The result was a 16 percent fall in California's lung cancer rate, compared with a drop of 2.7 percent in the rest of the U.S.

Smoking other drugs

Drugs are chemical substances that cause changes in the mind or the body. Many drugs are used legally for medicinal purposes. Some drugs, such as tobacco, alcohol, and caffeine, are also legal but are used for recreational purposes. Other, "recreational" drugs, such as marijuana, heroin, ecstasy, and cocaine, are illegal because they are more dangerous, more addictive, or simply less acceptable to society than legal drugs are. However, tobacco is a far bigger killer than all other drugs combined.

▲ Marijuana smokers tend to inhale more deeply than smokers of conventional cigarettes.

Marijuana

Marijuana is made from the dried leaves of the marijuana plant. Like tobacco, it is usually smoked. It induces feelings of relaxation and euphoria, and its physical effects include increased pulse rate, mild pain reduction, and dizziness. It is not physically addictive. Evidence suggests that it has some medical benefits, including the relief of symptoms of multiple sclerosis, and there is a vigorous debate in many countries about whether or not it should be legalized. Some people argue that it should remain illegal because marijuana use might lead to the misuse of more dangerous drugs. They also say that not enough is known about the effects of marijuana—it may cause cancer in the same way as tobacco.

However, perhaps the biggest health concern is that marijuana is usually mixed with tobacco and smoked in hand-rolled cigarettes, or "joints," without a filter. Marijuana smokers also tend to inhale particularly deeply. Researchers say that smoking three marijuana cigarettes a day may be as dangerous as smoking 20 conventional cigarettes.

Crack cocaine

Crack is a smokable form of cocaine, which is extracted from the coca plant. When heated in a pipe, crack vaporizes and is easily inhaled. As with many drugs, it is highly addictive, and users can die from an overdose. Although crack does not contain the same substances found in tobacco, the smoke can seriously harm the lungs and cause chest pains. Crack is believed to be more rapidly addictive than other forms of cocaine because smoking it allows extremely high doses of the drug to reach the brain more quickly.

A man smokes crack cocaine with the aid of a small blowtorch.

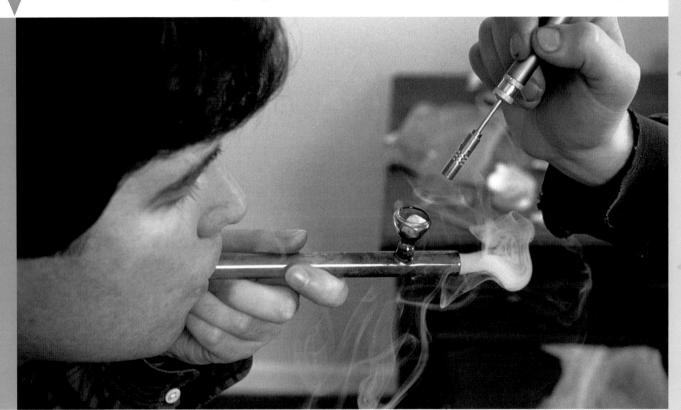

It's your experience

"No one I know thinks marijuana is dangerous. Some people are scared of drugs like heroin and crack, but marijuana is just like a cigarette. Most of our parents smoked it when they were younger, didn't they?"

Michael, age 15

It's your decision

What do statistics prove?
Statistics show that 63 percent of smokers have used illegal drugs, while only 1 percent of nonsmokers have used them. Some people argue that this proves that smoking leads to drug misuse. However, we can choose not to use illegal drugs, just as we can choose not to use tobacco products.

Quitting

Quitting smoking is not easy. In the U.S., nearly 60 percent of teenage smokers try to quit each year and fail. In Britain, nearly half of all smokers between the ages of 11 and 15 want to quit, yet almost two-thirds have failed on their first attempt. This is because they have become addicted to nicotine.

Quitting takes mental commitment and determination to confront the physical symptoms of nicotine withdrawal. Many people try several times before they quit smoking for good.

Having the support of someone who understands can boost our confidence and motivation to quit.

Motivation and support

No one else can make us quit smoking. Sometimes, being told that we ought to quit is not helpful because it can create feelings of failure and hopelessness. We have to want to do it for ourselves. Nevertheless, once we decide we want to quit, it is vital that we get as much support from family and friends as possible. This is particularly important in beating the mental addiction. If other people know what triggers our desire for a cigarette, they may be able to help us avoid those situations.

Some people prefer to go to a support group where they can share their experiences with people who understand what they are going through. Others try hypnosis or acupuncture, although there is no evidence to prove whether or not these treatments genuinely help.

It's your experience

"I always smoked my first cigarette of the day on the way to school. I couldn't give it up, but then I started biking instead of walking. It's difficult to smoke on a bike."

Jon, age 16

Nicotine patches release a controlled dose of nicotine into the body.

Physical aids

Many smokers find it difficult to quit using willpower alone. A number of products have been shown to increase success rates for quitters, but they can be expensive and are not available to everyone.

Nicotine replacement therapy, or NRT, is the most widely used aid. A range of patches, gums, and sprays delivers a low dose of nicotine without delivering the other harmful elements of tobacco smoke. The dose of nicotine is gradually reduced over a number of weeks until the user is completely free from dependence on nicotine.

Buproprion is an antidepressant drug available by prescription that attaches itself to the same receptors in the brain as nicotine. It prevents the user from going into nicotine withdrawal and lessens the urge to smoke. However, buproprion may, on rare occasions, cause seizures.

Exercise

Many people find exercise helpful because it releases endorphins into the brain that may disguise some of the effects of nicotine withdrawal.

It's your decision

Some people decide to smoke fewer cigarettes rather than quit smoking altogether. Smoking two cigarettes a day is better for us than smoking 20 cigarettes, but doctors point out that cutting down doesn't help us quit—it merely reinforces the cycle of craving.

The good news!

Thousands of people manage to stop smoking every day. If we quit smoking, we can undo much of the damage smoking has done to our health.

Health benefits

After only two days, there is no nicotine left in the body. After one year, the risk of heart attack falls to about half that of a smoker. Other benefits include younger-looking skin, whiter teeth, fresher breath, and more energy.

◀ Quitting smoking improves our energy levels by increasing the amount of oxygen we can absorb.

It's your experience

"I thought it would be easy to quit, but on the third day, I got really bored and had a cigarette. The next time I tried, I had an argument with my dad and gave in again. This time I'm going to do it. I know what to expect, and I don't want to be trying to stop all my life."

Carla, age 17

Time since quitting	Health benefits
20 minutes	Blood pressure and pulse rate return to normal.
8 hours	Oxygen levels return to normal.
24 hours	There is no carbon monoxide left in the body.
48 hours	There is no nicotine left in the body.
72 hours	Breathing becomes easier and energy levels increase.
One year	Risk of heart attack falls to half that of a smoker.

Help yourself

Most quitters find it useful to think carefully about ways in which cravings and difficult moments can be tackled and overcome. A plan of action might include some of the following:

QUITTING HELP LIST

If you have tried to stop in the past, think about what did and did not help.

Identify those moments when you most want a cigarette, and think about how you might deal with them. Is your first cigarette of the day the one you crave the most? Would a small change to your morning routine be helpful?

• Would it be easier for you to quit on a weekday or a weekend?

• Tell your friends that you are planning to quit so that they can offer support. If they are unlikely to be supportive, tell them you are not smoking because of a sore throat.

• Some people eat more and put on some extra weight when they quit smoking. Decide what to do about this in advance. You might choose to drink more water or to chew sugar-free gum.

• Have a list of support groups and hotline phone numbers on hand, ready for those difficult moments.

It's your opinion

Do you think it is better to tell everyone when you are planning to quit, or does this just make you feel worse if you fail?

What would you rather spend your money on?

Think of the money

Smoking costs a fortune. One of the best things about quitting is how much money you will save each month. Think about what it can be spent on, and plan on treating yourself!

Making a choice

Cigarettes are bad for our health. Yet for most of us, choosing whether or not to smoke is about far more than understanding addiction and the damage tobacco can do to our bodies. It is about fitting in, growing up, building an identity, and finding self-confidence. We all need to be aware of which issues are likely to influence our decision the most.

We don't need to smoke to have a good time.

It's your decision

Can you say "no"?
No one can tell you what to do. However, if you are worried about smoking, then practice saying "no" and give your reasons to a friend or even to the mirror. The more we say no to cigarettes, the more confident we become in ourselves as nonsmokers.

Self-image
At some point in our lives, most of us have a poor self-image. This might have to do with how attractive we feel or how many friends we have. Tobacco companies are very good at promoting their products as cool, glamorous, and sophisticated. Sometimes we hope that by smoking, we will transform into more desirable, interesting people. However, there are plenty of successful nonsmoking role models.

Peer pressure

Pressure from people around us to behave in a particular way can be hard to resist. If our friends smoke, it is difficult not to join in. Everyone needs to be accepted, and rejection is stressful for young people who are moving away from their parents and redefining their place in the world.

If peer pressure is a problem, it might be better to find different friends. If this is difficult, you could even make up a reason for not smoking, such as asthma.

Dealing with problems

Some people smoke as a way of dealing with boredom, stress, or loneliness. For these people, the psychological crutch of smoking can be difficult to overcome.

It is worth remembering that smoking does not actually remove our problems. At best, it may distract us for a minute, but it can add to feelings of stress or failure when addiction takes hold and we lose the ability to control our smoking habit.

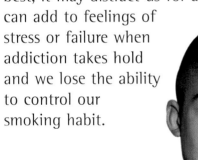

It's your opinion

According to the Tobacco Manufacturers Association, "Smoking is an adult pursuit and should remain a matter for informed and adult choice." Others argue that someone who is addicted to nicotine is no longer capable of exercising free choice about smoking. What do you think?

Many young smokers say they would prefer not to smoke.

It's your health!

If you are at an age when you are legally allowed to smoke, it is up to you to decide whether or not to smoke. It is an adult decision, based on whether you think the benefit of smoking is worth the risk to your health.

Have you made your choice?

Glossary

Acupuncture inserting needles into the skin to stimulate the body to heal itself

Addictive drug a drug that the body and mind can become dependent on

Additives substances such as preservatives and flavorings that are added to tobacco

Asthma a respiratory disease

Bronchitis inflammation of the airways

Buproprion an antidepressant drug that lessens the urge to smoke

Carbon monoxide a poisonous gas present in tobacco smoke

Crack a smokable form of the illegal drug cocaine

Dopamine a chemical in the brain associated with feelings of pleasure

Emphysema a lung disease

Hypnosis a therapy in which the subconscious mind is guided toward a desired outcome

Joint a hand-rolled cigarette made with marijuana

Low tar cigarettes with holes in the filter to allow air to mix with the smoke

Marijuana the dried leaves of the cannabis plant

Nicotine the addictive drug present in all tobacco products

Nicotine replacement therapy (NRT) patches, gums, or sprays that deliver a controlled dose of nicotine without the harmful effects of smoke

Nitrosamines powerful cancer-causing compounds present in all tobacco

Oral tobacco any kind of tobacco that is chewed in the mouth

Secondhand smoke the smoke from other people's cigarettes or cigars

Snuff powdered tobacco

Stimulant any drug that stimulates the central nervous system

Tar a harmful, brown, sticky substance found in cigarette smoke

Withdrawal symptoms feelings of anxiety, sleeplessness, or irritability that may be experienced by people who are trying to break a nicotine addiction

Further Information

American Cancer Society
A Web site that provides information about smoking and cancer.

www.cancer.org

Center for Disease Control
The Web site of the U.S. Center for Disease Control provides several resources to help people quit smoking.

www.cdc.gov/tobacco/how2quit.htm

FOREST (Freedom Organization for the Right to Enjoy Smoking Tobacco)
An organization that defends the interests of smokers and promotes freedom of choice.

www.forestonline.org

The Foundation for a Smokefree America
An organization dedicated to helping young people remain tobacco-free and helping smokers quit.

www.anti-smoking.org

Truth
An antitobacco organization with links to various facts about cigarettes and smoking.

www.thetruth.com

Campaign for Tobacco-Free Kids
A campaign to protect kids from the dangers of smoking and tobacco use.

www.tobaccofreekids.org

Note to parents and teachers: Every effort has been made to ensure that these Web sites are suitable for children, that they are of the highest educational value, and that they contain no inappropriate or offensive material. However, because of the nature of the Internet, it is impossible to guarantee that the contents of these sites will not be altered. We strongly advise that Internet access be supervised by a responsible adult.

Index